LETTERS OF NOTE: LOVE

Letters of Note was born in 2009 with the launch of lettersofnote.com, a website celebrating old-fashioned correspondence that has since been visited over 100 million times. The first *Letters of Note* volume was published in October 2013, followed later that year by the first Letters Live, an event at which world-class performers delivered remarkable letters to a live audience.

Since then, these two siblings have grown side by side, with *Letters of Note* becoming an international phenomenon, and Letters Live shows being staged at iconic venues around the world, from London's Royal Albert Hall to the theatre at the Ace Hotel in Los Angeles.

You can find out more at lettersofnote.com and letterslive.com. And now you can also listen to the audio editions of the new series of *Letters of Note*, read by an extraordinary cast drawn from the wealth of talent that regularly takes part in the acclaimed Letters Live shows.

Letters of Note

LOVE

Shaun Usher

For Karina

PENGUIN BOOKS
An imprint of Penguin Random House LLC
penguinrandomhouse.com

First published in Great Britain by Canongate Books Ltd 2020
Published in Penguin Books 2020

Compilation and introductions © 2020 by Shaun Usher

LIBRARY OF CONGRESS CATALOGING-IN-PUBLICATION DATA
Names: Usher, Shaun, 1978- editor.
Title: Letters of note. Love / compiled by Shaun Usher.
Other titles: Love
Description: New York : Penguin Books, 2020. |
Identifiers: LCCN 2020026493 (print) |
LCCN 2020026494 (ebook) | ISBN 9780143134633 (paperback) |
ISBN 9780525506447 (ebook)
Subjects: LCSH: Love-letters.
Classification: LCC PN6140.L7 L393 2020 (print) |
LCC PN6140.L7 (ebook) |
DDC 808.86/93543--dc23
LC record available at https://lccn.loc.gov/2020026493
LC ebook record available at https://lccn.loc.gov/2020026494

Printed in the United States of America
1   3   5   7   9   10   8   6   4   2

Set in Joanna MT

CONTENTS

A letter is a time bomb, a message in a bottle, a spell, a cry for help, a story, an expression of concern, a ladle of love, a way to connect through words. This simple and brilliantly democratic art form remains a potent means of communication and, regardless of whatever technological revolution we are in the middle of, the letter lives and, like literature, it always will.

INTRODUCTION

Nothing in life holds as much power as love. It is the force that binds us. In our darkest moments, during the toughest of times, the ever-present pull of love demands that we persevere and gives us the strength necessary to keep going. Indeed, consumed by love, connected to another human being at such a fundamental level, one feels ready and able to achieve anything; to overcome any obstacle that life would dare place in one's way; to fight to the death, if necessary, in an effort to protect all that is held close to one's heart.

Love, I would argue, is the nearest thing we have to a superpower. But with highs come lows, and a love that has soured can swiftly and without compromise bring someone to their knees, devastating the very life it once enriched. The unremitting, overwhelming pain that can fill the vacuum left by a love lost is unlike any other feeling, its effects almost impossible to articulate. It is life without colour. A movie with no sound. To fully surrender yourself to love is to lower all defences, and the fact that we continue to pursue love despite such enormous emotional risk is testament to its immeasurable benefits.

It is no surprise, then, that the letter, our most private form of communication, has proven to be such a popular medium through which to send and discuss love, a special *something* that is difficult to define on the page, despite being described by many as our only truly universal language. In this volume can be found a selection of letters that go some way towards illustrating our complex relationship with this alluring energy, including a letter of advice from parent to lovesick child, which contains words of wisdom surely valuable for people of all ages, and the letter that led to the striking down of a ban on mixed-race marriages in the United States, written by a lady with a surname so perfect as to be almost unbelievable. You will also read an acutely unromantic marriage proposal from 1866, which may induce tears of laughter and a long sigh of pity, and a desperate letter from a broken-hearted escaped slave to the man who helped him flee his master, in which he seeks assistance in finding his beloved wife. And, of course, you will find numerous examples of the trusty love letter – letters to lovers, letters to the dead, letters unsent – a form of correspondence with no modern equivalent, and a flavour of letter to which millions of people, myself included, owe so much.

It was in September of 2002 that my obsession with letters first reared its head, provoked by a long-distance correspondence with a new friend who had no option but to move hundreds of miles away and set up home, albeit for just ten months. The phrase 'social media' was yet to be uttered, and at that point in time, email still seemed exotic, so our decision to keep in touch by 'old-fashioned letter' sounded almost normal. What we had not anticipated was just how enjoyable and insightful those letters would be, and how perfect a start our blossoming relationship had been given.

Karina and I married in 2012. This book is for her.

Shaun Usher
2020

The Letters

LETTER 01
NOTHING GOOD GETS AWAY
John Steinbeck to Thom Steinbeck
10 November 1958

Born in California in 1902, John Steinbeck remains a giant in the world of fiction thanks to his classic novels The Grapes of Wrath, East of Eden *and* Of Mice and Men. *Additionally, when he reached sixty, his standing was further cemented when he was awarded the Nobel Prize for Literature, an honour bestowed on so few. As was the case with most authors in the 1950s, Steinbeck was a keen letter writer who enjoyed the to and fro: he kept up correspondence with all manner of people, from fellow authors through to US presidents, with effortless style. In 1958, four years before the big award, Steinbeck wrote arguably his best, and certainly most valuable, letter, to his fourteen-year-old son. At the time, Thomas was at boarding school and had fallen for a girl. He needed some fatherly advice.*

THE LETTER

Dear Thom,

We had your letter this morning. I will answer it from my point of view and of course Elaine will from hers.

First—if you are in love—that's a good thing— that's about the best thing that can happen to anyone. Don't let anyone make it small or light to you.

Second—There are several kinds of love. One is a selfish, mean, grasping, egotistical thing which uses love for self-importance. This is the ugly and crippling kind. The other is an outpouring of everything good in you—of kindness and consideration and respect—not only the social respect of manners but the greater respect which is recognition of another person as unique and valuable. The first kind can make you sick and small and weak but the second can release in you strength, and courage and goodness and even wisdom you didn't know you had.

You say this is not puppy love. If you feel so deeply—of course it isn't puppy love.

But I don't think you were asking me what you feel. You know better than anyone. What you wanted me to help you with is what to do about it—and that I can tell you.

Glory in it for one thing and be very glad and grateful for it.

The object of love is the best and most beautiful. Try to live up to it.

If you love someone—there is no possible harm in saying so—only you must remember that some people are very shy and sometimes the saying must take that shyness into consideration.

Girls have a way of knowing or feeling what you feel, but they usually like to hear it also.

It sometimes happens that what you feel is not returned for one reason or another—but that does not make your feeling less valuable and good.

Lastly, I know your feeling because I have it and I'm glad you have it.

We will be glad to meet Susan. She will be very welcome. But Elaine will make all such arrangements because that is her province and she will be very glad to. She knows about love too and maybe she can give you more help than I can.

And don't worry about losing. If it is right, it

happens—The main thing is not to hurry. Nothing good gets away.

Love,

Fa

LETTER 02
I CANNOT DO LESS
Simone de Beauvoir to Nelson Algren
10 September 1950

*French philosophers Simone de Beauvoir and Jean-Paul
Sartre spent much of their lives together, in a complex
and extraordinary relationship that lasted for fifty-one
years, until Sartre's death in 1980. Other partners came
and went over the years, but in 1947 Simone met
Nelson Algren, a novelist she found impossible to
resist, despite the long distance between them, and
with whom she would correspond for eighteen years.
In 1950, on her return home from a loveless trip to
Nelson's city of Chicago that clearly signalled the end
of the affair she had so enjoyed, Simone wrote him a
letter.*

THE LETTER

Hotel Lincoln, New York
30 Septembre 1950

Nelson, my dearest sweetest one,
You had just left when a man came smiling and
gave me this beautiful crazy flower, with the two
little birds and the love from Nelson. that nearly
spoilt my fine behaviour: it was hard to "weep no
more." Yet, I am better at dry sadness than at cold
anger, for I remained dry eyed until now, as dry as
smoked fish, but my heart is a kind of dirty soft
custard inside. I waited for an hour and a half at
the airport, because of the weather; the plane from
Los Angeles had not been able to land in this fog. It
was right that you went away; this last waiting is
always too long, but it was good that you had
come. Thanks for the flower and for coming, not to
speak of the other things. So I waited with the
purple flower on my breast, pretending to read the
MacDonald mystery, and then we took off. The trip
was very easy—no tossing at all. I did not sleep but
pretended to read the mystery to the end, and kept
fondling you in my dirty, silly heart.

New York was a beauty: hot, sunny, and grey at
the same time. What a glamorous city! I did not

want to break my heart by going to the Brittany. I picked the Lincoln where I had landed three years ago, when I knew nobody in this whole continent and did not suspect I should be so strangely trapped in Chicago. I got exactly the same room I had, a little nearer the sky, but identical. How queer to find myself in this faraway past again! As I did three years ago, I went to Lincoln beauty shop: no trouble either, the hotel seems empty, the beauty shop empty. Then I bought the pen for Olga, which was fourteen, so I am glad you gave me so much dollars; I'll just make it. And I walked and walked in the town, along this Third Avenue, which we walked thoroughly down the last night, two years ago, all around the Brittany, too, and once more I found you everywhere and reminded everything. I wandered in Washington park where they have a kind of flea-market and bad painting sale; I went up the Fifth Avenue bus and saw the night come down on New York.

Now it is nine, I just had a little sandwich since the plane, no sleep since Wabansia; I am awfully tired. I came to my room to write to you and drink scotch. But I don't think I can go to bed now. I feel New York around me, behind me our summer. I'll go to bed now. I'll go down and walk and dream around, until I am utterly exhausted.

I am not sad. Rather stunned, very far away from myself, not really believing you are now so far, so far, you so near. I want to tell you only two things before leaving, and then I'll not speak about it any more, I promise. First, I hope so much, I want and need so much to see you again, some day. But, remember, please, I shall never more ask to see you— not from any pride since I have none with you, as you know, but our meeting will mean something only when you wish it. So, I'll wait. When you'll wish it, just tell. I shall not assume that you love me anew, not even that you have to sleep with me, and we have not to stay together such a long time—just as you feel, and when you feel. But know that I'll always long for your asking me. No, I cannot think that I shall not see you again. I have lost your love and it was (it is) painful, but shall not lose you. Anyhow, you gave me so much, Nelson, what you gave me meant so much, that you could never take it back. And then your tender-ness and friendship were so precious to me that I can still feel warm and happy and harshly grateful when I look at you inside me. I do hope this tenderness and friendship will never, never desert me. As for me, it is baffling to say so and I feel ashamed, but it is the only true truth: I just love you as much as I did when I landed into your disappointed arms, that means with my whole self and all my dirty heart; I cannot do less. But that will not bother you, honey, and don't make writing letters any kind of a duty, just write when you feel like it, knowing every time it will make me very happy.

Well, all words seem silly. You seem so near, so near, let me come near to you, too. And let me, as in the past times, let me be in my own heart forever.

Your own Simone

LETTER 03
KNOW THAT YOU ARE LOVED
Dorothy Freeman to Rachel Carson
December 1963

In 1953, nine years before the publication of her
groundbreaking and immeasurably important exposé
Silent Spring, *pioneering marine biologist Rachel Carson*
received a letter from a fan named Dorothy Freeman
that kick-started a decade-long correspondence through
which they developed a deep bond. Their letters
touched on every imaginable subject, and they spoke
openly about love. Ten years after that first contact
was made, four months before Carson died from a
heart attack brought on by the cancer she had fought
for some time, Freeman sent her dear friend her
annual Christmas letter – the last she was ever able to
address to Carson.

THE LETTER

Dearest Rachel,

Ten years, dear, since that first Christmas message.
What can I say now, ten years later, that I didn't say
in 1953? The words may be different but the
theme – I need you, I love you – is the same. As I
needed you then for understanding, and for the
kind of companionship that no one else has been
able to give, I need you now as much, and even
more. As I loved you then, for yourself, and for all
you represent, I love you now – with warmth and
earnestness and longing.

And so I give my Christmas thanks for this ten
years – years that have enriched, yes, and even
changed my life. Such years – of joy and sorrow
for us both. As we shared the joys, no less have we
shared the sorrows. Sometimes I wonder how I
could have endured the depths without your
sustaining love. Without you, in those shadowy
days I know life would not have been worth living.

But I must not remember the darkness to-night.
What I remember is the loveliness that has been
mine because of you: the shared beauties of Nature
in all its forms; the world of books and the people
in that world; the companionship in music; but
above all the living inspiration of you. For all this

and so much more that words cannot express, my gratefulness knows no bounds. I can always reach into my memory for a lovely moment – if I tried to catalogue them I should never stop.

Yesterday at twilight the cloudless western sky was aglow with the burning orange which is at its best when seen through the dark silhouette of the spruces of our Maine forest. The diamond brilliance of the evening star was still an hour high. Below it was the first faint shimmering crescent of the young moon which is to be the Christmas moon – and which (oh, joy to be) we may share. At its tip a star punctuated the scene! No need to tell you of what happened in my eyes. There is promise in that moon for it reaches its full on Dec. 30.

Whatever time it is when you read this, please know my arms are figuratively about you. So close your eyes and know that you are loved.

May your Christmas be a blessed one.

With all my love always,

Dorothy

LETTER 04
MY SOUL IS VEXED
Isaac Forman to William Still
7 May 1854

In December of 1853, twenty-three-year-old Isaac Forman grasped a rare opportunity to say goodbye to a life of slavery in Norfolk, Virginia, by fleeing to Toronto in Canada. He left behind his slave owner of many years, Mrs Sanders. However, to his great dismay, Forman also left behind his wife; enslaved, too, but to a different owner, in Richmond. Little trace of Isaac Forman's life remains. Thanks to this letter, though, we can be certain that he found life without his beloved quite unbearable. It was sent to William Still, a famous conductor on the Underground Railroad, a secret network of people, places and routes through which thousands of slaves, Forman included, escaped slavery.

THE LETTER

TORONTO,
May 7, 1854.

MR. W. STILL: — Dear Sir — I take this opportunity
of writing you these few lines and hope when they
reach you they will find you well. I would have
written you before, but I was waiting to hear from
my friend, Mr. Brown. I judge his business has
been of importance as the occasion why he has not
written before. Dear sir, nothing would have
prevented me from writing, in a case of this kind,
except death.

My soul is vexed, my troubles are inexpressible.
I often feel as if I were willing to die. I must see
my wife in short, if not, I will die. What would I
not give no tongue can utter. Just to gaze on her
sweet lips one moment I would be willing to die
the next. I am determined to see her some time or
other. The thought of being a slave again is miserable. I hope heaven will smile upon me again,
before I am one again. I will leave Canada again
shortly, but I don't name the place that I go, it may
be in the bottom of the ocean. If I had known as
much before I left, as I do now, I would never have
left until I could have found means to have brought

her with me. You have never suffered from being absent from a wife, as I have. I consider that to be nearly superior to death, and hope you will do all you can for me, and inquire from your friends if nothing can be done for me. Please write to me immediately on receipt of this, and say something that will cheer up my drooping spirits. You will oblige me by seeing Mr. Brown and ask him if he would oblige me by going to Richmond and see my wife, and see what arrangements he could make with her, and I would be willing to pay all his expenses there and back. Please to see both Mr. Bagnel and Mr. Minkins, and ask them if they have seen my wife. I am determined to see her, if I die the next moment. I can say I was once happy, but never will be again, until I see her; because what is freedom to me, when I know that my wife is in slavery? Those persons that you shipped a few weeks ago, remained at St. Catherine, instead of coming over to Toronto. I sent you two letters last week and I hope you will please attend to them. The post-office is shut, so I enclose the money to pay the post, and please write me in haste.

I remain evermore your obedient servant,

I. FORMAN.

'I MUST SEE MY WIFE
IN SHORT, IF NOT, I
WILL DIE.'

— Isaac Forman

LETTER 05
YOU ARE SUPERIOR TO ALL
Juliette Drouet to Victor Hugo
1835

By the time of her death in 1883, French actress Juliette Drouet had been the mistress of Les Misérables novelist Victor Hugo for fifty years. They met behind the scenes of his play Lucrezia Borgia, in which she was starring, in 1833, at which point Hugo's wife, Adèle Foucher, was having an affair with literary critic Charles Augustin Sainte-Beuve. Hugo therefore felt no qualms about embarking on his own affair with Drouet. During that half-century, Drouet devoted herself entirely to Hugo and wrote to him every single day – on many days she wrote more than once. Tens of thousands of her letters survived, of which this is just one.

THE LETTER

Friday 8 p.m.

If I were a clever woman, my gorgeous bird, I could describe to you how you unite in yourself the beauties of form, plumage, and song! I would tell you that you are the greatest marvel of all ages, and I should only be speaking the simple truth. But to put all this into suitable words, my superb one, I should require a voice far more harmonious than that which is bestowed upon my species—for I am the humble owl that you mocked at only lately. Therefore, it cannot be. I will not tell you to what degree you are dazzling and resplendent. I leave that to the birds of sweet song who, as you know, are none the less beautiful and appreciative.

I am content to delegate to them the duty of watching, listening and admiring, while to myself I reserve the right of loving; this may be less attractive to the ear, but it is sweeter far to the heart. I love you, I love you, my Victor; I can not reiterate it too often; I can never express it as much as I feel it.

I recognise *you* in all the beauty that surrounds me—in form, in colour, in perfume, in harmonious sound: all of these mean *you* to me. You are superior to them all. You are not only the solar spectrum with the seven luminous colours, but the sun himself, that illumines, warms, and revivifies the whole world! That is what you are, and I am the lowly woman who adores you.

Juliette

LETTER 06
I HAVE NEVER LOVED BEFORE AS I LOVE YOU

Vladimir Nabokov to Véra Slonim
8 November 1923

Vladimir Nabokov and Véra Slonim's fifty-year relation-
ship was a fascinating one. Both born in Saint
Petersburg, Russia – he in 1899, she three years later –
he claimed it was at a ball in Berlin in 1923 that they
first met, her face covered by a harlequin mask as she
recited one of his poems from memory. They married
two years later. While Nabokov concentrated on
writing some of the greatest fiction known to man,
Slonim worked as his sounding board, his muse, his
editor, his agent, his translator, his chauffeur, his
manager and, it is said, his handgun-wielding body-
guard. She even plucked from a fire the manuscript of
his opus Lolita, which on more than one occasion was
almost destroyed by her doubt-ridden husband. She
was everything to him, and he to her, and Nabokov's
many love letters to his wife brim with adoration. This
fine example was penned months after their first
meeting.

THE LETTER

TO: 41, Landhausstrasse,
Berlin W.
8–XI–23

How can I explain to you, my happiness, my
golden, wonderful happiness, how much I am all
yours – with all my memories, poems, outbursts,
inner whirlwinds? Or explain that I cannot write a
word without hearing how you will pronounce it –
and can't recall a single trifle I've lived through
without regret – so sharp! – that we haven't lived
through it together – whether it's the most, the
most personal, intransmissible – or only some
sunset or other at the bend of a road – you see
what I mean, my happiness?

And I know: I can't tell you anything in words –
and when I do on the phone then it comes out
completely wrong. Because with you one needs to
talk wonderfully, the way we talk with people long
gone, do you know what I mean, in terms of
purity and lightness and spiritual precision – but I
– *je patauge* terribly. Yet you can be bruised by an
ugly diminutive – because you are so absolutely
resonant – like seawater, my lovely.

I swear – and the inkblot has nothing to do

with it — I swear by all that's dear to me, all I
believe in — I swear that I have never loved before
as I love you, — with such tenderness — to the
point of tears — and with such a sense of radiance.
On this page, my love, I once began to write a
poem for you and this very inconvenient little tail
got left — I've lost my footing. But there's no other
paper. And most of all I want you to be happy and
it seems to me that I could give you that happiness
— a sunny, simple happiness — and not an altogether
common one.

And you should forgive me for my pettiness —
that I am thinking with aversion about how —
practically — I will mail this letter tomorrow — and
yet I am ready to give you all of my blood, if I had
to — it's hard to explain — sounds flat — but that's
how it is. Here, I'll tell you — with my love I could
have filled ten centuries of fire, songs, and valour —
ten whole centuries, enormous and winged, — full
of knights riding up blazing hills — and legends
about giants — and fierce Troys — and orange sails —
and pirates — and poets. And this is not literature
since if you reread carefully you will see that the
knights have turned out to be fat.

No — I simply want to tell you that somehow I
can't imagine life without you — in spite of your
thinking that it is 'fun' for me not to see you for

two days. And you know, it turns out that it wasn't Edison at all who thought up the telephone but some other American, a quiet little man whose name no one remembers. It serves him right.

Listen, my happiness — you won't say again that I'm torturing you? How I'd like to take you off somewhere with me — you know how those highwaymen of old did: a wide-brimmed hat, a black mask, and a bell-shaped musket. I love you, I want you, I need you unbearably . . . Your eyes — which shine so wonder-struck when, with your head thrown back, you tell something funny — your eyes, your voice, lips, your shoulders — so light, sunny . . .

You came into my life — not as one comes to visit (you know, 'not taking one's hat off') but as one comes to a kingdom where all the rivers have been waiting for your reflection, all the roads, for your steps. Fate wanted to correct its mistake — as if it has asked my forgiveness for all of its previous deceptions. So how can I leave you, my fairy-tale, my sun? You see, if I'd loved you less, then I would have had to go. But this way — it makes no sense. And I don't want to die, either. There are two kinds of 'come what may'. Involuntary and deliberate. Forgive me — but I live by the second one. And you can't take away my faith in what I am afraid to

think about – it would have been such happiness
. . . And here's another little tail.

Yes: an old-fashioned slowness of speech, steely simplicity . . .
Thus the heart's more ardent: steel, incandesced by flight . . .

This is a fragment of my long poem – but didn't
go in it. Wrote it down once, so not to forget, and
here it is now – a splinter.

All of this I'm writing lying in bed, resting the
page on a huge book. When I work long into the
night, the eyes of one of the portraits on the wall
(some great-grandmother of our landlord) become
intent and very unpleasant. So good to have
reached the end of this little tail, such a nuisance.

My love, good night . . .

Don't know whether you'll be able to make
sense of this illiterate letter . . . But never mind . . .
I love you. Will wait for you tomorrow at 11 p.m.
– otherwise call me after 9.

V.

LETTER 07
WE FORMED ONLY ONE BEING
Maud Gonne to W.B. Yeats
26 July 1908

Nobel Prize-winning poet W.B. Yeats proposed to Irish actress and activist Maud Gonne four times in the space of a decade – in 1891, 1899, 1900 and 1901 – and each time, to his dismay, she declined. To make matters worse, she then, in 1903, dispelled the notion that marriage may have been the problem, by accepting a proposal from another man, a Major John MacBride. Still, they remained close, and Gonne was something of a muse for Yeats through the years, inspiring some of his poetry. They also shared an interest in the occult, and in July of 1908, a few months before their relationship was finally consummated, Maud wrote him a letter.

THE LETTER

Willie

It is not in a week but in a day that I am writing
you. I had such a wonderful experience last night
that I must know at once if it affected you & how?
for above all I don't want to do any thing which
will take you from your work, or make working
more arduous – That play is going to be a
wonderful thing & must come first – nothing must
interfere with it.

Last night all my household had retired at a
quarter to 11 and I thought I would go to you
astrally. It was not working hours for you & I
thought by going to you I might even be able to
leave with you some of my vitality & energy which
would make working less of a toil next day – I had
seen the day before when waking from sleep a
curious some what Egyptian form floating over me
(like in the picture of Blake the soul leaving the
body) – It was dressed in moth like garments &
had curious wings edged with gold in which it
could fold itself up – I had thought it was myself,
a body in which I could go out into the astral – at

27

a quarter to 11 last night I put on this body & thought strongly of you & desired to go to you.

We went some where in space I don't know where – I was conscious of starlight & of hearing the sea below us. You had taken the form I think of a great serpent, but I am not quite sure. I only saw your face distinctly & as I looked into your eyes (as I did the day in Paris you asked me what I was thinking of) & your lips touched mine. We melted into one another till we formed only *one being, a being greater than ourselves* who felt all & knew all with double intensity – the clock striking 11 broke the spell & as we separated it felt as if life was being drawn away from me through my chest with almost physical pain. I went again twice, each time it was the same – each time I was brought back by some slight noise in the house. Then I went upstairs to bed & I dreamed of you confused dreams of ordinary life. We were in Italy together (I think this was from some word in your letter which I had read again before sleeping). We were quite happy, & we talked of this wonderful spiritual vision I have described – you said it would tend to increase physical desire – This troubles me a little – for there was nothing physical in that union – Material union is but a pale shadow compared to it – write to me quickly & tell me if you know anything of

this & what you think of it – & if I may come to
you again like this. I shall not until I hear from
you. My thought with you always.

Maud Gonne

LETTER 08
I HAVE HAD MY EYE ON YOU
Simon Fallowfield to Mary Foster
29 November 1866

*On 29 November 1866, in the Yorkshire village of
Middlesmoor, a middle-aged farmer by the name of
Simon Fallowfield plucked up the courage to propose
marriage – not in person, but by letter, and not to
someone he knew particularly well – to a young local
lady named Mary Foster who had, for her sins,
repeatedly caught his eye. It is little surprise to learn
that Mary declined Simon's most generous offer.
Whether his Plan B was effective is another question
altogether.*

THE LETTER

My Dear Miss,

I now take up my pen to write to you hoping
these few lines will find you well as it leaves me at
present Thank God for it. You will perhaps be
surprised that I should make so bold as to write to
you who is such a lady and I hope you will not be
vex at me for it. I hardly dare say what I want, I
am so timid about ladies, and my heart trimmels
like a hespin. But I once seed in a book that faint
heart never won fair lady, so here goes.

I am a farmer in a small way and my age is
rather more than forty years and my mother lives
with me and keeps my house, and she has been
very poorly lately and cannot stir about much and I
think I should be more comfortabler with a wife.

I have had my eye on you a long time and I
think you are a very nice young woman and one
that would make me happy if only you think so.
We keep a servant girl to milk three kye and do the
work in the house, and she goes out a bit in the
summer to gadder wickens and she snags a few of
turnips in the back kend. I do a piece of work on
the farm myself and attends Pately Market, and I
sometimes show a few sheep and I feeds between
3 & 4 pigs agen Christmas, and the same is very

useful in the house to make pies and cakes and so forth, and I sells the hams to help pay for the barley meal.

I have about 73 pund in Naisbro Bank and we have a nice little parlour downstairs with a blue carpet, and an oven on the side of the fireplace and the old woman on the other side smoking. The Golden Rules claimed up on the walls above the long settle, and you could sit all day in the easy chair and knit and mend my kytles and leggums, and you could make the tea ready agin I come in, and you could make butter for Pately Market, and I would drive you to church every Sunday in the spring cart, and I would do all that bees in my power to make you happy. So I hope to hear from you. I am in desprit and Yurnest, and will marry you at May Day, or if my mother dies afore I shall want you afore. If only you will accept of me, my dear, we could be very happy together.

I hope you will let me know your mind by return of post, and if you are favourable I will come up to scratch. So no more at present from your well wisher and true love—

Simon Fallowfield

P.S. I hope you will say nothing about this. If you will not accept of me I have another very nice

woman in my eye, and I think shall marry her if
you do not accept of me, but I thought you would
suit me mother better, she being very crusty at
times. So I tell you now before you come, she will
be Maister.

LETTER 09
I WEEP AND WEEP AND WEEP
Nadezhda Mandelstam to Osip Mandelstam
22 October 1938

On 13 May 1934, almost a year after reciting to some friends a satirical poem he had written on the subject of Stalin, one of the most important Russian poets of the era, Osip Mandelstam, was arrested. Luckily, he was saved from execution, and instead, upon his release, he and his wife, Nadezhda, were forced to live in exile in the Russian city of Voronezh. Their luck ran out in 1938 when the poet was arrested for a second time, and on this occasion sent to the forced labour camp in which he would eventually die. In October of 1938, two months before his death, his wife wrote him this letter. Nadezhda continued to live in exile and was unable to return to Moscow for another twenty-six years. She was finally able to tell their story in her 1970 memoir, Hope Against Hope.

THE LETTER

22 OCTOBER 1938

Osia, my beloved, faraway sweetheart!
I have no words, my darling, to write this letter
that you may never read, perhaps. I am writing it
into empty space. Perhaps you will come back and
not find me here. Then this will be all you have left
to remember me by.

Osia, what a joy it was living together like
children — all our squabbles and arguments, the
games we played, and our love. Now I do not even
look at the sky. If I see a cloud, who can I show it
to?

Remember the way we brought back provi-
sions to make our poor feasts in all the places
where we pitched our tent like nomads?
Remember the good taste of bread when we got
it by a miracle and ate it together? And our last
winter in Voronezh. Our happy poverty, and the
poetry you wrote. I remember the time we were
coming back once from the baths, when we
bought some eggs or sausage, and a cart went
by loaded with hay. It was still cold and I was
freezing in my short jacket (but nothing like
what we must suffer now: I know how cold

35

you are). That day comes back to me now. I understand so clearly, and ache from the pain of it, that those winter days with all their troubles were the greatest and last happiness to be granted us in life.

My every thought is about you. My every tear and every smile is for you. I bless every day and every hour of our bitter life together, my sweetheart, my companion, my blind guide in life.

Like two blind puppies we were, nuzzling each other and feeling so good together. And how fevered your poor head was, and how madly we frittered away the days of our life. What joy it was, and how we always knew what joy it was.

Life can last so long. How hard and long for each of us to die alone. Can this fate be for us who are inseparable? Puppies and children, did we deserve this? Did you deserve this, my angel? Everything goes on as before. I know nothing. Yet I know everything – each day and hour of your life are plain and clear to me as in a delirium.

You came to me every night in my sleep, and I kept asking what had happened, but you did not reply.

In my last dream I was buying food for you in a filthy hotel restaurant. The people with me were total strangers. When I had bought it, I realized I did not know where to take it, because I do not know where you are.

When I woke up, I said to Shura: 'Osia is dead.' I do not know whether you are still alive, but from the time of that dream, I have lost track of you. I do not know where you are. Will you hear me? Do you know how much I love you? I could never tell you how much I love you. I cannot tell you even now. I speak only to you, only to you. You are with me always, and I who was such a wild and angry one and never learned to weep simple tears – now I weep and weep and weep.

It's me: Nadia. Where are you?

Farewell.

Nadia

LETTER 10
GO RIGHT AHEAD AND GET MARRIED
Zora Neale Hurston to Herbert Sheen
7 May 1953

In 1920, while studying at Howard University in Washington, D.C., twenty-nine-year-old author and soon-to-be 'Queen of the Harlem Renaissance' Zora Neale Hurston met Herbert Sheen, a jazz pianist six years her junior with whom she quickly began to spend much of her time. They fell in love, and in 1927 became husband and wife, but four years later decided to go their separate ways, choosing to remain close friends throughout their lives and subsequent marriages. They corresponded regularly, and in 1953 Sheen made Hurston aware of his current relationship troubles: he was now looking to leave his second wife, Quinlock, and instead marry a 'young lady'. This was Hurston's response.

THE LETTER

Eau Gallie, Fla.
May 7, 1953.

Dear Herbert

Oh I do thank you for the suggestion about the
"anxiety" help. How did you know that I needed
something like that? Did you make the diagnosis
from my letters, or just probably thought that I
might need it? You are a wonderful doctor.

Your conclusions about the reactions of the
church dignitaries is clearly analytical. Yes, they are
very and only human after all. They could not
admit that they might have been wrong years ago
at Tyler Texas. "Authority" is very precious to the
hierarchy and they will not abate one jot or tittle
of it easily. The priest there has probably been
convinced that yours is a King Henry VIII case, and
is dealing with it accordingly. I hear that Quinlock
accuses you of getting too big for your britches
since financial success came to you, and bent on
crushing any and all who dare to oppose you. She
has no doubt wept that out to the church fathers.
Just in case that it has not been expounded to you,
the Rota in Rome, whose authority passes on
divorce, take the stand that the only real grounds

on which they can grant a divorce is that one party entered into the marriage with no intention of making it a real marriage, in other words, insincerely. For other reasons than a "holy" union. Keep that in mind when you approach Monsignor Fulton J. Sheen. I have never met him, but Claire Boothe Luce has discussed him to me. From what is said of him you have a better chance of being understood than with the small fry. He is abreast of the times instead of being ardently traditional.

Today Mr. Burch of the firm of Van G. Werley brought me the abstract to read, 41 pages going back to the time when Florida belonged to Spain and on down to 1953. The title is clear and there are no liens against the property except the taxes for 1953 which will not be due until November 1, 1953. $16.50. The contract has gone to Thomas R. Barr, Jr. at Fort Pierce for his signature and I will have a copy in a week at the latest. Then I will send it along to you for your inspection. The firm is strong for me to develop it into a housing project, but at present I think that I would like it better to plant it to an acre of fancy mangoes and perhaps five acres of oranges. The demand for orange juice concentrates seems inexhaustible and the price is good. Since concentrates were discovered they can be shipped so easily all over the nation and abroad without loss that fruit is really booming. The big companies leave your grove and take care of everything.

It's none of my business really, but if I were you, I would not be deterred by the ban of the church. I would go right ahead and get married if that is what you want. A ten-ton truck might run over Quinlock's head some day and then you could re-marry in the church. For my money, priests are only men and without your experience in the world and with women. They rule from theory, not practice and have no more intimate acquaintance with God than you have. I still believe that the Roman Catholic church is the greatest institution that man has ever invented for human spiritual comfort on the average, but I have never lost track of the fact that it is human. Priests have lectured me on my intellectual approach instead of trusting all and everything to faith which my mental set-up will not allow.

To me, Herbert, the concept of God being that He is both omnipotent and omniscient, that He should want humans to know certain things and to be guided by these principles and reveal it to so few. Why cannot His will be as freely revealed since it is so important? And why allow Himself to be so easily misconstrued? Why so many religions? Why "reveal" Himself to an Arab in one light and to a Caucasian in another? And to a Hindu in still another and to a Mongol in still another? No, I cannot go for that. To me those divergent views are evidence of humanity groping after the divine concept, each in his own way in the absence of any definite proof anywhere. I have no belief in any bearded divinity sitting on a cloud. That is an anthropomorphic concept entirely human. God made in man's own image. To me there is LAW to which all things in the universe must conform. What the explanation of it is, I do not know, though I would like to know. We are confusing human social arrangements with divinity. I cannot conceive of Law caring whether you "go forth and multiply" with Quinlock or with "the young lady". You cannot deny the command within your own body to commit the act of reproducing your kind, for that has not been obscured by human theories, (which to me proves my contention that LAW makes itself very clear and definite where it is concerned) and is not concerned with human social conveniences, for that is what it amounts to. Marriage and social laws were evolved primarily to protect children and the mothers of children, and that is that. Do not deny yourself the woman you want in this life in the belief that you will get her as a reward in Heaven. I have not been there, but somebody whispered to me that angels have no business in the marriage bed, having no sex organs. Maybe that is why cherubs are nothing but heads. See where that will bring you out? You and the "young lady" will meet as heads with wings under your chins in the hereafter. But what fun is that? The Moslem heaven is much more exciting where male spirits are surrounded by beautiful women. Houris. But as you know, they do not even wait for that, but take full advantage of what is available here and now. That is a much more realistic religion. It goes along with nature instead of inventing sins to suffer for. Human beings invented sin, not God. Very religious people are either sadists or masochists, and sometimes both. They like to suffer and castigate themselves and know a horrid frenzy when you do not suffer likewise and set out to make you feel their vengeance, too. The famed affair of Heloise and Abelard is tragic to me only in that they were so chuckled-headed in spending all that time accusing themselves instead of her throwing off her veil and his stepping on out of that monastery and going about their business. People waste too much time worrying about whether an affair will last. Enjoy it while it does last and then suffer no regrets later. That is the fundamental difference between Quinlock and myself. I look back upon my experience with you as a time of pleasure without regrets. She is full of bitterness and vengeance because it did not keep on lasting. Love should not last beyond the point where it is pleasurable. Ergo, she is not capable of love but only a possessive frenzy. That passes for love with many people. "I killed him because I love him."

Here's luck to your day of freedom!
Sincerely
Zora

'PEOPLE WASTE TOO
MUCH TIME WORRYING
ABOUT WHETHER AN
AFFAIR WILL LAST.
ENJOY IT WHILE IT DOES
LAST AND THEN SUFFER
NO REGRETS LATER.'

— Zora Neale Hurston

LETTER 11
YOU WILL NEVER BE FAR AWAY
Marina Tsvetaeva to Rainer Maria Rilke
1926/7

Leading poets Rainer Maria Rilke and Marina
Tsvetaeva never met in person, and they corresponded
for just eight months, yet their letters somehow reveal
a deep bond. They were introduced, by mail, in April of
1926 by fellow poet Boris Pasternak: Rilke's first letter
to Tsvetaeva was accompanied by signed copies of his
work, to which she responded, 'You are the very incar-
nation of poetry.' Before long he was sending freshly
crafted poetry, written just for her. But their love
was never able to blossom fully, as on 29 December
of the same year, Rilke died of leukaemia – a battle
he had been fighting for some time and about which he
had warned Tsvetaeva. Two days after his death, she
began writing one final letter to Rilke, never to be
sent. It was completed two months later.

THE LETTER

Bellevue
December 31, 1926–February 8, 1927.

The year ended in your death? The end? The
beginning! You yourself are the New Year. (Beloved,
I know you are reading this before I write it.) I am
crying, Rainer, you are streaming from my eyes!

Dear one, now that you are dead there is no
death (or no life!). What can I say? That little town
in Savoy — when? where? Rainer, what about that
"nest" to keep our dreams in? Now Russian is an
open book to you, so you know that the Russian
word for "nest" is *gnezdo*. And you know so many
other things.

I don't want to reread your letter or I will want
to join you — there — and I dare not wish for such
a thing. You know what such a wish implies.

Rainer, I am always conscious of your presence
at my shoulder.

Did you ever think of me? Yes, of course you
did.

Tomorrow is New Year's Day, Rainer. 1927. Seven
is your favourite number. You were born in 1875
(newspaper date?). Fifty-one years old?

How disconsolate I am!

Don't dare to grieve! At midnight tonight I will drink with you (you know how I clink glasses – ever so lightly!).

Beloved, come to me often in my dreams. Live in my dreams. Now you have a right to wish and to fulfill your wishes.

You and I never believed in our meeting here on earth, any more than we believed in life on this earth, isn't that so? You – have gone before me (and that is better!), and to receive me well you have taken not a room, not a house, but a whole landscape. I kiss you . . . on the lips? on the temple? on the forehead? Of course on the lips, for real, as if alive.

Beloved, love me more and differently from others. Don't be angry with me. You must grow accustomed to me, to such a one as I am. What else?

No, you are not yet far away and high above, you are right here, with your head on my shoulder. You will never be far away: never inaccessibly high.

You are my darling grown-up boy.

Rainer, write to me! (A foolish request?)

Happy New Year and may you enjoy the heavenly landscape!

Marina

Rainer, you are still on this earth; twenty-four hours have not yet passed.

LETTER 12
IMMORTAL BELOVED

Ludwig van Beethoven to his 'Immortal Beloved'
July 1812

German composer Ludwig van Beethoven was fifty-six
years of age when he passed away in March 1827,
leaving behind not just an enduring musical legacy but
also what would become one of history's most famous
and hotly debated love letters. It was discovered by a
friend shortly after his death, in a secret drawer
hidden in Beethoven's wardrobe, along with some other
personal papers, and is undated: thanks to the paper's
watermark, however, we know that it was written in
1812. It was also, it seems, unsent, and written over
the course of two days while he recuperated from an
illness in the Czech city of Teplice. The letter's unnamed
recipient – Beethoven's 'Immortal Beloved' – remains a
mystery.

THE LETTER

My angel, my all, my own self — only a few
words today, and that too with pencil (with yours)
— only till tomorrow is my lodging definitely
fixed. What abominable waste of time in such
things — why this deep grief, where necessity
speaks?

Can our love persist otherwise than through
sacrifices, than by not demanding everything? Canst
thou change it, that thou are not entirely mine, I
not entirely thine? Oh, God, look into beautiful
Nature and compose your mind to the inevitable.
Love demands everything and is quite right, so it is
for me with you, for you with me — only you
forget so easily, that I must live for you and for me
— were we quite united, you would notice this
painful feeling as little as I should . . .

. . . We shall probably soon meet, even today I
cannot communicate my remarks to you, which
during these days I made about my life — were
our hearts close together, I should probably not
make any such remarks. My bosom is full, to tell
you much — there are moments when I find that
speech is nothing at all. Brighten up — remain

my true and only treasure, my all, as I to you. The rest the gods must send, what must be for us and shall.

Your faithful
Ludwig

Monday evening, 6 July

You suffer, you, my dearest creature. Just now I perceive that letters must be posted first thing early. Mondays — Thursdays — the only days, when the post goes from here to K. You suffer — oh! Where I am, you are with me, with me and you, I shall arrange that I may live with you. What a life!

So! Without you — pursued by the kindness of the people here and there, whom I mean — to desire to earn just as little as they earn — humility of man towards men — it pains me — and when I regard myself in connection with the Universe, what I am, and what he is — whom one calls the greatest — and yet — there lies herein again the godlike of man. I weep when I think you will probably only receive on Saturday the first news from me — as you too love — yet I love you stronger — but never hide yourself from me. Good night — as I am taking the waters, I must go to

bed. Oh God — so near! so far! Is it not a real
building of heaven, our Love — but as firm, too, as
the citadel of heaven.

Good morning, on 7 July

Even in bed my ideas yearn towards you, my
Immortal Beloved, here and there joyfully, then
again sadly, awaiting from Fate, whether it will
listen to us. I can only live, either altogether with
you or not at all. Yes, I have determined to wander
about for so long far away, until I can fly into
your arms and call myself quite at home with
you, can send my soul enveloped by yours into
the realm of spirits — yes, I regret, it must be.
You will get over it all the more as you know my
faithfulness to you; never another one can own
my heart, never — never! O God, why must one
go away from what one loves so, and yet my life
in W. as it is now is a miserable life. Your love
made me the happiest and unhappiest at the same
time. At my actual age I should need some conti-
nuity, sameness of life — can that exist under our
circumstances? Angel, I just hear that the post
goes out every day — and must close therefore, so
that you get the L. at once. Be calm — love me
— today — yesterday.

What longing in tears for you — You — my Life
— my All — farewell. Oh, go on loving me —
never doubt the faithfullest heart
Of your beloved
L

Ever thine.
Ever mine.
Ever ours.

LETTER 13
I FEEL HAPPY TONIGHT
Anne Lindbergh to Charles Lindbergh
2 July 1944

On 2 July 1944, as she travelled by train from Chicago to San Francisco, author and aviator Anne Morrow Lindbergh wrote the following letter to her husband, Charles Lindbergh – an aviation pioneer who, seventeen years previously, flew from New York to Paris in the Spirit of St. Louis *to much acclaim. They remained married until Charles's death in 1974, by which time they had both had extramarital affairs and Charles had fathered several children by women other than his wife. They had also dealt with the kidnapping and murder of one of their six children – their twenty-month-old son, Charles Jr – despite intense, previously unrivalled media coverage in what was dubbed 'the trial of the century'.*

THE LETTER

July 2nd, Train Chicago — San Francisco

Dear Charles,

I am on my way West. I hope to meet you. I feel
madly extravagant and altogether quite mad,
speeding over the country with not much certainty
of when or where I'll meet you.

But I feel happy tonight. I have sat and watched
the cornfields of Iowa darken, seen the homesteads
pass by—a white house, a red barn and a brave
cluster of green trees in the midst of oceans of flat
fields—like an oasis in a desert. The glossy flanks of
horses and the glossy leaves of corn. And I have
been overcome by the beauty and richness of this
country I have flown over so many times with you.
And overcome with the beauty and richness of our
life together, those early mornings setting out,
those evenings gleaming with rivers and lakes
below us, still holding the last light. Those fields of
daisies we landed on—and dusty fields and desert
stretches. Memories of many skies and many earths
beneath us—many days, many nights of stars.
"How are the waters of the world sweet—if we
should die, we have drunk them. If we should
sin—or separate—if we should fail or secede—we

have tasted of happiness—we must be written in the book of the blessed. We have had what life could give, we have eaten of the tree of knowledge, we have known—we have been the mystery of the universe."

Good night—

Anne

'I HAVE BEEN
OVERCOME BY THE
BEAUTY AND RICHNESS
OF THIS COUNTRY I
HAVE FLOWN OVER SO
MANY TIMES WITH YOU'
— *Anne Lindbergh*

LETTER 14
THIS IS A LOVE LETTER, IS IT NOT?
John Jay Chapman to Minna Timmins
21 September 1892

Born in New York in 1862, poet John Jay Chapman was twenty-five years old when he punished astronomer Percival Lowell with a cane for mistreating Chapman's girlfriend and future wife, Minna Timmins. On later discovering that Lowell was in fact innocent of said charge, Chapman punished himself by thrusting his own hand in a fire, burning it so severely that amputation was the only option. Rather than flee after such madness, Timmins instead married Chapman the next year, and in 1892 he wrote her this love letter – one of many they exchanged until her death in 1898 during childbirth.

THE LETTER

Littleton,
Colorado,
21st September 1892

I have sealed up each one of these letters thinking I
had done—and then a wave of happiness has come
over me—remembering you—only you, my
Minna—and the joy of life. Where were you, since
the beginning of the world? But now you are here,
about me in every space, room, sunlight, with your
heart and arms and the light of your soul—and the
strong vigor your presence. It was not a waste
desert in Colorado. It is not a waste time, for you
are here and many lives packed into one life, and
the green shoot out of the heart of the plant,
springing up blossoms in the night, and many old
things have put on immortality and lost things have
come back knocking within, from before the time I
was conceived in the womb, there were you also.
And what shall we say of the pain! it was false—
and the rending, it was necessary. It was the
breaking down of the dams that ought not to have
been put up—but being up it was the sweeping
away of them that the waters might flow together.

This is a love letter, is it not? How long is it since

I have written you a love letter, my love, my Minna? Was the spring hidden that now comes bubbling up overflowing curb and coping-stone, washing my feet and my knees and my whole self? How are the waters of the world sweet—if we should die, we have drunk them. If we should sin—or separate—if we should fail or secede—we have tasted of happiness—we must be written in the book of the blessed. We have had what life could give, we have eaten of the tree of knowledge, we have known—we have been the mystery of the universe.

Is love a hand or a foot—is it a picture or a poem or a fireside—is it a compact or a permission or eagles that meet in the clouds—No, no, no, no. It is light and heat and hand and foot and ego. If I take the wings of the morning and remain in the uttermost parts of the sea there art thou also—He descended into Hell and on the third day rose again—and there art thou also—in the lust or business—in the stumbling and dry places, in sickness and health—every sort of sickness there also—what matter is it what else the world contains—if you only are in it in every part of it? I can find no corner of it without you—my eyes would not see it. It is empty—I have seen all that is there and it is nothing, and over creation are your wings.

Have we not lived three years now together—and

daily nearer—grafted till the very sap of existence
flows and circulates between us—till I know as I
write this—your thoughts—till I know as a feeling, a
hope, a thought, passes through me—it is yours?
Why the agony of those old expressions and attempts
to come by diligent, nervous, steady, fixing of the eye
on the graver's tool, as if the prize depended on
drawing it straight, those pounds of paper and nights
of passionate composition—did they indeed so well
do their work that the goal was carried—or was it
the silent communion—of the night—even after days
of littleness or quarrel that knitted us together? It
does not matter, love, which it was. It put your soul
so into my body that I don't speak to you to convey
meaning. I write only for joy and happiness. How
diligently have we set fact to fact and consideration
against consideration during the past years—as if we
were playing dominoes for our life. How cloudy I
have been—dragging you down, often nailing useless
nails cutting up and dissecting, labeling, crucifying
small things—and there was our great love over us,
growing, spreading—I wonder we do not shine—or
speak with every gesture and accent giving messages
from the infinite—like a Sibyl of Michael Angelo. I
wonder people do not look after us in the street as if
they had seen an angel.

    Tuo Giovanni.

LETTER 15
I LOVE MY WIFE. MY WIFE IS DEAD.
Richard Feynman to Arline Feynman
17 October 1946

Nobel Prize-winning physicist Richard Feynman was one of the most remarkable scientists of the twentieth century and a key figure in many notable scientific advances, including the development of the atomic bomb as a member of the Manhattan Project. But he wasn't just a great intellect: he had charisma, and an uncanny ability to impart this wealth of previously impenetrable knowledge to the general public in terms they could understand. When he died of cancer aged sixty-nine, a leading light really did go out. It was around this time, after his death, that a love letter was discovered in his belongings, addressed to his beloved wife, Arline. It was written in October of 1946, sixteen months after she had passed away following a battle with tuberculosis. His daughter, Michelle, has said of this particular missive, 'This letter is well worn – much more so than others – and it appears as though he reread it often.'

THE LETTER

D'Arline,

I adore you, sweetheart.

I know how much you like to hear that—but I don't only write it because you like it—I write it because it makes me warm all over inside to write it to you.

It is such a terribly long time since I last wrote to you—almost two years but I know you'll excuse me because you understand how I am, stubborn and realistic; and I thought there was no sense to writing.

But now I know my darling wife that it is right to do what I have delayed in doing, and that I have done so much in the past. I want to tell you I love you. I want to love you. I always will love you.

I find it hard to understand in my mind what it means to love you after you are dead—but I still want to comfort and take care of you—and I want you to love me and care for me. I want to have problems to discuss with you—I want to do little projects with you. I never thought until just now that we can do that. What should we do.

We started to learn to make clothes together—or learn Chinese—or getting a movie projector. Can't I do something now? No. I am alone without you and you were the "idea-woman" and general instigator of all our wild adventures.

When you were sick you worried because you could not give me something that you wanted to and thought I needed. You needn't have worried. Just as I told you then there was no real need because I loved you in so many ways so much. And now it is clearly even more true— you can give me nothing now yet I love you so that you stand in my way of loving anyone else—but I want you to stand there. You, dead, are so much better than anyone else alive.

I know you will assure me that I am foolish and that you want me to have full happiness and don't want to be in my way. I'll bet you are surprised that I don't even have a girlfriend (except you, sweetheart) after two years. But you can't help it, darling, nor can I—I don't understand it, for I have met many girls and very nice ones and I don't want to remain alone—but in two or three meetings they all seem ashes. You only are left to me. You are real.

My darling wife, I do adore you.
I love my wife. My wife is dead.
Rich.

PS Please excuse my not mailing this—but I don't know your new address.

MY ANGEL, MY LOVE
Emilie Blachère to Rémi Ochlik
2012

Born in France in 1983, Rémi Ochlik knew from a young age that photography was to be his lifelong passion. As a photojournalist, he began to make a name for himself by covering the Haitian riots in 2004; seven years later he won awards for his work documenting the Arab Spring. But with each assignment, he sensed his personal safety was increasingly at risk. Tragically, in 2012, as he travelled around Syria reporting on the civil war, Ochlik was killed when a rocket hit the safe house in which he was taking shelter. Soon after his death, his heartbroken partner, Emilie, wrote him a letter.

THE LETTER

Ochlik,

I've never found it so difficult to write. My dictionaries are useless. I can already hear you saying, "Sweet Blachère." So instead I made a list of everything I loved about you.

My angel, my love:

I loved it when you made lists of things you wanted, and you wanted a Harley Davidson, a loft, a 22,000-euro titanium Leica, and you would say to me, "What? You work at Paris Match, don't you?"

I loved it when you called me Blachère, or Blacherounette, when you had something you wanted to ask me.

I loved it that you wanted to find a country just for the two of us where we could go every year together on assignment.

I loved it when you talked about the arts, and painting, and literature, and I couldn't understand a thing. You taught me so much.

I loved it how in the field you would sink into the shadows, making people forget you were there so you could take better pictures.

I loved to see you look every morning at photo sites and hear you say, "Look at what they're doing. I suck, Blachère."

I loved it when you recorded L'amour est dans le pré for us and we watched it curled up under a blanket like teenagers, with our kitten between us. You kept saying, "You better not tell anyone about this."

I loved watching you make me coffee every morning, and after eight months, it was actually good!

I loved it when you said you wanted to have two children, a boy and a girl.

I loved it even more when you pestered me in front our friends about having kids: "Look at Thib, Mat, Fred. Their girls are cool, and they're pregnant!"

I loved it that you decided you wanted to go to Libya, Nigeria and Burma, then Syria, then Tulles, all within five minutes.

I loved it when you told me, "Blachère, you're making me childish. I'm becoming like you."

I loved it when I said that you were the best photographer in the world and you said, "Well, you're biased."

I loved to see you blush when I told you I was crazy about you.

I loved our routine, our life together, the nights we'd stay up late watching Dexter. I was smiling so long as I was next to you.

I loved it how at night you would take out your

contact lenses and put on your thick glasses. I'd call you Harry Potter and you hated it. You called me Emilie.

I loved it when you told me that you didn't miss me at all.

I loved it when you told me you were jealous of Eric, of Ivan, of Pierre, jealous of everyone, even Marcelle, my cat.

I loved it when you kidnapped Marcelle when I was on assignment and took her home so she would get used to your cat, and we could all live together, one happy family.

I loved it when you were scared to meet my mother.

I loved it when you took me to Honfleur, and we stopped along the highway and ate a Mars bar and drank a Coke.

I loved it when you told me, "I'm ugly, Blachère, you're blinded by love."

I loved it when you left your toothbrush at my house. I took a picture of it and showed it to my girlfriends. I almost posted it on Facebook.

I loved how stroked my leg at red lights on your scooter.

I loved it how you held me tight in the morning, then again at night, as if we had been apart for months.

I loved watching you smoke at the window. You were so sexy. But like you said, I'm biased.

I loved to hear you say to Julien, your best friend, your brother, "Look out, Mama Squirrel's here," when I was waking up.

I loved it when you said at first, "Julien's my wife, you're my mistress." After two months, it was the opposite. Sorry, Julien.

I loved your timid smile, the way you laughed, your almost feminine delicacy, your juvenile tenderness.

I loved it how you texted me every five minutes to ask me to marry you, with emoticons and all. We promised each other we'd get hitched in Las Vegas.

I loved it how you left me love letters in my notebooks when you came over to feed Marcelle.

I loved your courage, your admiration, your rigor. I'm so proud of you, my angel. I admired you as a photojournalist and as a man. You've become so big.

I loved it when you told me, "Blachère, we have our whole lives ahead of us."

I loved to hear you tell me how everything was going to be alright when I was depressed. If only I could hear you tell me that today.

I loved it so much how on February 10, a

Friday, the last time we saw each other, you told me that I made you happy.

I could go on. I would have loved to spend my life adding to this list. Ochlik, I loved you. I hope you know up there that I was more than happy by your side. I was in bloom. With you, things were lovely, sweet, and surprisingly intense. Our time together was magic. We were so happy that we had to protect it from the invasions of our profession, our passion, our second love.

We were prepared for everything, except for the worst. Ochlik, I don't know how I can go on without you. In Rome, you told me, "love is a weakness." You were wrong. Today I feel strong. At Christmas you gave me a notebook and told me to, "write down the story of our lives and read it to our kids." I promise that I will tell the story of that life we dreamed of so often, a life that I'm now going to have to live for two.

I'm not sure if you miss me, Ochlik. I miss you. Madly.

But I know that you are here. Inside of me. Near me. Near us. Today our nickname, Blachlik, makes sense.

One day I'll join you, my love. But not yet. You would hate to see me give up, let myself fade away. So I'm drying my tears, and watching your favorite movies on repeat, the ones that made you happy, like Singin' in the Rain.

I'm sure you'd rather see us pay you tribute by staying up all night drinking and smoking. Don't worry, it will happen, and the night's not over yet.

My angel, give Lucas a kiss for me. Take care of yourself. Take care of us.

Emilie Blachère

'I PROMISE THAT I WILL
TELL THE STORY OF
THAT LIFE WE DREAMED
OF SO OFTEN'

— Emilie Blachère

LETTER 17
A PROBLEM WE HAVE
Mildred Loving to the American Civil Liberties
Union
20 June 1963

In 1958, five weeks after marrying in the District of
Columbia, Mildred and Richard Loving, a mixed-race
couple from Virginia, were arrested at their home for
violating the state's Racial Integrity Act of 1924. Rather
than separate, the Lovings moved to Washington, D.C.,
where such a union was permitted by law; however,
before long they grew homesick. In June of 1963,
Mildred wrote a letter to Attorney General Robert F.
Kennedy and asked him to step in: he advised them to
send this letter to the American Civil Liberties Union,
which led to a lawsuit and the landmark decision of
Loving v. Virginia, 388 U.S. 1 (1967). *On 12 June 1967,*
thanks to the Lovings' efforts, US-wide laws that
denied interracial couples the right to marry were
deemed unconstitutional following a unanimous deci-
sion at the United States Supreme Court.

THE LETTER

1151 Neal Street
N.E. Wash. D.C.
June 20, 1963

Dear Sir:

I am writing to you concerning a problem we have.

5 yrs ago my husband and I were married here in the District. We then returned to Va. to live. My husband is White, I am part negro, & part indian.

At the time we did not know there was a law in Va. against mixed marriages.

Therefore we were jailed and tried in a little town of Bowling Green.

We were to leave the state to make our home.

The problem is we are not allowed to visit our families. The judge said if we enter the state within the next 30 yrs, that we would have to spend 1 yr in jail.

We know we can't live there, but we would like to go back once in awhile to visit our families & friends.

We have 3 children and cannot afford an attorney.

We wrote to the Attorney General, he suggested that we get in touch with you for advice.

Please help us if you can. Hope to hear from you real soon.

Yours truly,

Mr. & Mrs. Richard Loving

LETTER 18
PIECES OF MEAT TO HUNGRE WOLFE
Addie Brown to Rebecca Primus
24 May 1861

In 1994, one side of a years-long correspondence was discovered, and later published, which ignited debate amongst scholars due to the romantic relationship the letters seemed to reveal. They were written by Addie Brown, a lady born in 1841 who was orphaned as a young child following the death of her father and subsequently brought up by her aunt in Philadelphia. With no formal education to speak of, she went on to work as a domestic servant throughout her adult life. The letters' recipient was Rebecca Primus, a woman who, in contrast to Brown, was the eldest of four children in an affluent, middle-class Connecticut family and worked as a highly respected teacher. Their lives were very different in many ways; however, like Brown, she was also a woman of colour. It is not known how they met, nor is it clear how Primus responded to Brown's frequent, often heated declarations of love. What is clear is that this Civil War-era relationship was unlike most others. While Brown's lack of literacy can mean her letters are, at times, tricky to make sense of word for word, the emotion behind her writing is impossible to mistake.

THE LETTER

New York May 24 1861

My Darling Rebecca
your most Affec letter to me was like pieces of
meat to hungre wolfe I will not tell how often I
pursue the contents of it this eve for the first time
since I left that I gave vent to tears O Dear Dear
Rebecca no one knows the heart of your Dear
Friend I am afraid I will become irksom to the
Family they say I am a change girl in every way
I will try and be agreeable as I can how can I
when you are so far off. I'm thinking of you
hourly.

Dear Rebecca if I had the energy of the dove
how swiftly I would fly to the arms of my love.

Dear Rebeca Mother has a great deal of work in
the house I'm very much pleased for that I must
have something to occupying my mind Rebecca
what do you think Mr. Lee has here turn to me he
has been expecate his Affec towards me but I act so
indifferently that he dont know what to make of
me I like him as a Friend and nothing more then
that but Dear Rebecca if I should ever see a good
chance I will take it for I'm tired roving around
this unfriendly world Dear Rebecca in all this do

not forget what I have said about marrying do not
mention what I'm about to pen to you my true
Friend that is this I do believe by Mr. Lee action
that he truly loves me I cannot reciprocate his love
he ask me if I thought that I ever live in Hartford
again. I told him did not know he said I thought I
would.

Rebecca what do you think my old lover come
home from church with me stay sun AM the. . .
to stir a little in my breast dont laugh at me my
Darling. Mother has two gentlemen boarded and
one of them has partly fell in love with me
mother told him and also Selina that no chance
for him now Dear Rebecca mother says she did
not think I was so dear to her I must say she is
very Affectionately to me but if it only be lasting
dont you say so to my love as for my part I try
not to be changeable although I leave that for you
to judge.

Rebecca where do you think Mrs. Nott will go
when she dies for I think she is not. . . live please
to forgive me for saying so but that is true she
know just as well as she was a living that she did
not give me but one shirt and then she hardly
wanted to then but I would persist in having it she
wanted to send it down there I know I now have it
then so I made shure of it then Rebecca I dont

think I ever shall make my home again with Mrs. Nott because I dont think Mrs. Nott no kind of a woman to be with Im almost disgusted with her.

Dear Rebecca we have deep bereavement in the Family Mother only Friend is dead he has been a Father to her he has staid by in all her trouble if she wanted anything would always go to him and him only he has been a near Dear Friend to this Family Rebecca it heart rendering to see his widow I saw him for the last time on Sunday he was apparently in perfect good health and very lively indeed Monday AM Mother was sent for and thought he would choke to death but they work for over him he seem to much better mother come home at 2 o'clock PM thought he would get along mother went in the evening to see he was great deal better so she came home at 1 o'clock she sent for and he was dying before Mother got up there he was dead O Rebecca how suddenly that was we all are very much afraid that Mrs. Scott will live very long now both are old and she is so nearing. . . that was the Family I thought to live with Rebecca I must bring this long letter to a close for I dont think will be very interesting to you if I only exchange this pen and paper for a seat by my loving Rebecca it is possible and must

be thus seperation how long how long <u>God</u> knows
and he only my heart is breaking for you and only
you good night from your sweet

    Affec.

    Addie

PS give my love to your Dear Mother and all the
rest of the Family give my love to your Aunt Em
and all the rest of the Friend Addie

LETTER 19
YOU ARE SPLENDID
Robert Schumann to Clara Wieck
1838

Celebrated German composer and pianist Robert Schumann first met and fell in love with fellow musical prodigy Clara Wieck whilst receiving piano training from her father, Friedrich Wieck, a man who actively discouraged their union and refused to give his daughter away to a 'penniless composer'. Undeterred, Schumann took the matter to court and, after a lengthy court battle, won the right to marry the lady who in 1840 would become his wife. Robert passed away in 1856, and Clara died 40 years later. They were survived by their eight children and countless heart-warming letters so infused with love that their battle to become wed can easily be understood.

THE LETTER

Clara,

How happy your last letters have made me – those
since Christmas Eve! I should like to call you by all
the endearing epithets, and yet I can find no love-
lier word than the simple word 'dear,' but there is a
particular way of saying it. My dear one, then, I
have wept for joy to think that you are mine, and
often wonder if I deserve you.

One would think that no one man's heart and
brain could stand all the things that are crowded
into one day. Where do these thousands of
thoughts, wishes, sorrows, joys and hopes come
from? Day in, day out, the procession goes on. But
how light-hearted I was yesterday and the day
before! There shone out of your letters so noble a
spirit, such faith, such a wealth of love!

What would I not do for love of you, my own
Clara! The knights of old were better off; they
could go through fire or slay dragons to win their
ladies, but we of today have to content ourselves
with more prosaic methods, such as smoking
fewer cigars, and the like. After all, though, we

can love, knights or no knights; and so, as ever, only the times change, not men's hearts . . .

You cannot think how your letter has raised and strengthened me . . . You are splendid, and I have much more reason to be proud of you than you of me. I have made up my mind, though, to read all your wishes in your face. Then you will think, even though you don't say it, that your Robert is a really good sort, that he is entirely yours, and he loves you more than words can say.

You shall indeed have cause to think so in the happy future. I still see you as you looked in your little cap that last evening. I still hear you call me du. Clara, I heard nothing of what you said but that du. Don't you remember?

But I see you in many another unforgettable guise. Once you were in a black dress, going to the theatre with Emilia List; it was during our separation. I know you will not have forgotten; it is vivid with me. Another time you were walking in the Thomasgasschen with an umbrella up, and you avoided me in desperation. And yet another time, as you were putting on your hat after a concert, our eyes happened to meet, and yours were full of the old unchanging love.

I picture you in all sorts of ways, as I have seen you since. I did not look at you much, but you charmed me so immeasurably. Ah, I can never praise you enough for yourself or for your love of me, which I don't really deserve.

Robert

LETTER 20
I'M TERRIBLY IN LOVE WITH YOU
James Schuyler to John Button
Spring 1956

James Schuyler was born in Chicago in 1923 and had a disjointed upbringing. His parents divorced early on, and as a result, much of his childhood was spent travelling the country with his mother and stepfather in search of a permanent home. As a young adult he briefly served in the US Navy, and in later life spent time in a New York mental institution having suffered the first of numerous breakdowns. Through it all, Schuyler wrote poetry, and in 1981, age fifty-seven, he was awarded the Pulitzer Prize for his collection, The Morning of the Poem. In the early 1950s Schuyler met and fell for painter John Button. They wrote to each other often.

'I LOVE BEING IN LOVE
WITH YOU, IT MAKES
EVEN UNHAPPINESS
SEEM NO BIGGER
THAN A PIN'

— James Schuyler

LETTER 21
LOOK FOR ME IN THE SUNSETS
Emmie to Sumner

Date unknown

There are more than 90,000 people buried at Mount Auburn Cemetery, a beautiful and sprawling garden cemetery in Massachusetts that was first opened in 1831. Carved into one of those gravestones is the text of a letter, written by a lady to the love she left behind.

THE LETTER

My Sweet Sumner,

I am very sorry that I had to go, it was simply my time. You were always the stronger of us. I could never had held the tiller for you as you did for me in such dark and ravaging seas. In my days of passage you were, as I knew you would be, perfect.

I have left the stage but I will never leave you. I am in a thousand places that will always be ours. Look for me in the sunsets, the ones that marry the light of a yawning day to the bright pink billowed clouds of a western sky. These are my sunsets not yours. Live my sweet Sumner, live with every ounce of love that you still have to give. Do not question this hunger that still rides within your warm and pounding heart.

If you get lonely just look for me. I am there in the sunset, listen closely and I will whisper my blessing.

Forever Your Valentine,

Emmie

LETTER 22
A LOUSY PROPOSITION
Evelyn Waugh to Laura Herbert
Spring 1936

Brideshead Revisited **novelist Evelyn Waugh was born in London in 1903, and in June 1928, three months prior to publication of his acclaimed debut** Decline and Fall **and with little money to speak of, he married his first wife, Evelyn Gardner – much to the annoyance of her unimpressed father. Within a year of the wedding, Waugh had filed for divorce. Years later, in the spring of 1936, as he waited impatiently for the annulment of his first marriage, he wrote to his soon-to-be-ex-wife's nineteen-year-old cousin, Laura, with a self-described 'lousy proposition'. This painfully honest, amusing approach paid off: Evelyn and Laura married the next year and remained together until his death thirty years later. They had seven children together.**

THE LETTER

Bridgewater Estate Office
Ellesmere
Salop

Sweetie,

Another letter last night. It is noble of you.

Tell you what you might do while you are alone
at Pixton. You might think about me a bit &
whether you could bear the idea of marrying me.
Of course you haven't got to decide, but think
about it. I can't advise you in my favour because I
think it would be beastly for you, but think how
nice it would be for me. I am restless & moody &
misanthropic & lazy & have no money except what
I earn and if I got ill you would starve. In fact it's a
lousy proposition. On the other hand I think I
could reform & become quite strict about not
getting drunk and I am pretty sure I should be
faithful. Also there is always a fair chance that there
will be another bigger economic crash in which
case if you had married a nobleman with a great
house you might find yourself starving, while I am
very clever and could probably earn a living of
some sort somewhere. Also though you would be
taking on an elderly buffer, I am one without fixed

habits. You wouldn't find yourself confined to any particular place or group. Also I have practically no living relatives except one brother whom I scarcely know. You would not find yourself involved in a large family & all their rows & you would not be patronised & interfered with by odious sisters in law & aunts as often happens. All these are very small advantages compared with the awfulness of my character. I have always tried to be nice to you and you may have got it into your head that I am nice really, but that is all rot. It is only to you & for you. I am jealous & impatient – but there is no point in going into a whole list of my vices. You are a critical girl and I've no doubt that you know them all and a great many I don't know myself. But the point I wanted to make is that if you marry most people, you are marrying a great number of objects & other people as well, well, if you marry me there is nothing else involved, and that is an advantage as well as a disadvantage. My only tie of any kind is my work. That means that for several months each year we shall have to separate or you would have to share some very lonely place with me. But apart from that we could do what we liked & go where we liked – and if you married a soldier or stockbroker or member of parliament or master of hounds you would be more tied.

When I tell my friends that I am in love with a girl of 19 they looked shocked and say 'wretched child' but I don't look on you as very young even in your beauty and I don't think there is any sense in the line that you cannot possibly commit yourself to a decision that affects your whole life for years yet. But anyway there is no point in your deciding or even answering. I may never get free of your cousin. Above all things, darling, don't fret at all. But just turn the matter over in your dear head.

Eight days from now I shall be with you again, darling heart. I don't think of much else.

All my love,

Evelyn

LETTER 23
I KNOW WHAT LOVE IS
Ansel Adams to Cedric Wright
10 June 1937

Born in 1902 in California, from an early age Ansel Adams was fascinated by nature and spent much of his time exploring the wide expanses of land that surrounded him. But it was when he reached twelve and got his hands on his first camera that he found his true passion, immediately planting the seeds that were to catapult him to stardom as one of the most famous landscape photographers in history. Sadly, in 1936, in the midst of an unrelenting workload and the near-demise of his marriage, Adams suffered a nervous breakdown. After a stay in hospital, desperately in need of escape, Adams decided he must return with his family to the one place where he could find solace: Yosemite, California. Some months later, as his health returned, he wrote a letter to his best friend and mentor, the photographer Cedric Wright.

THE LETTER

Dear Cedric,

A strange thing happened to me today. I saw a big thundercloud move down over Half Dome, and it was so big and clear and brilliant that it made me see many things that were drifting around inside of me; things that related to those who are loved and those who are real friends.

For the first time I know what love is; what friends are; and what art should be.

Love is a seeking for a way of life; the way that cannot be followed alone; the resonance of all spiritual and physical things. Children are not only of flesh and blood — children may be ideas, thoughts, emotions. The person of the one who is loved is a form composed of a myriad mirrors reflecting and illuminating the powers and the thoughts and the emotions that are within you, and flashing another kind of light from within. No words or deeds may encompass it.

Friendship is another form of love — more passive perhaps, but full of the transmitting and

acceptances of things like thunderclouds and grass
and the clean reality of granite.

Art is both love and friendship, and understanding; the desire to give. It is not charity, which
is the giving of Things, it is more than kindness
which is the giving of self. It is both the taking
and giving of beauty, the turning out to the light
the inner folds of the awareness of the spirit. It
is the recreation on another plane of the realities of
the world; the tragic and wonderful realities of
earth and men, and of all the inter-relations of
these.

I wish the thundercloud had moved up over
Tahoe and let loose on you; I could wish you
nothing finer.

Ansel

'LOVE IS A SEEKING FOR
A WAY OF LIFE; THE WAY
THAT CANNOT BE
FOLLOWED ALONE; THE
RESONANCE OF ALL
SPIRITUAL AND
PHYSICAL THINGS'

— Ansel Adams

LETTER 24
I'M AMPUTATING YOU
Frida Kahlo to Diego Rivera
1953

It was in 1927 that Frida Kahlo first met Diego Rivera,
a fellow artist twenty-one years her senior who soon
became her mentor and husband. Kahlo's life up until
then had been a struggle – she was bedridden with
polio as a child and suffered a serious traffic accident
as a young adult, which led to problems throughout
her adult life – but she pulled through thanks to her
love of art. As an adult she thrived, going on to
become one of the world's most admired painters, and
Rivera was similarly celebrated. Their marriage was
famously wild and unpredictable. In 1953, the year
before she died, one of Kahlo's legs was amputated
due to gangrene. As she waited for the operation to
take place, she wrote Rivera a letter.

THE LETTER

My dear Mr. Diego,

I'm writing this letter from a hospital room before
I am admitted into the operating theatre. They
want me to hurry, but I am determined to finish
writing first, as I don't want to leave anything
unfinished. Especially now that I know what they
are up to. They want to hurt my pride by cutting a
leg off. When they told me it would be necessary
to amputate, the news didn't affect me the way
everybody expected. No, I was already a maimed
woman when I lost you, again, for the umpteenth
time maybe, and still I survived.

I am not afraid of pain and you know it. It is
almost inherent to my being, although I confess that
I suffered, and a great deal, when you cheated on
me, every time you did it, not just with my sister
but with so many other women. How did they let
themselves be fooled by you? You believe I was
furious about Cristina, but today I confess that it
wasn't because of her. It was because of me and you.
First of all because of me, since I've never been able
to understand what you looked and look for, what

they give you that I couldn't. Let's not fool ourselves, Diego, I gave you everything that is humanly possible to offer and we both know that. But still, how the hell do you manage to seduce so many women when you're such an ugly son of a bitch?

The reason why I'm writing is not to accuse you of anything more than we've already accused each other of in this and however many more bloody lives. It's because I'm having a leg cut off (damned thing, it got what it wanted in the end). I told you I've counted myself as incomplete for a long time, but why the fuck does everybody else need to know about it too? Now my fragmentation will be obvious for everyone to see, for you to see . . . That's why I'm telling you before you hear it on the grapevine. Forgive my not going to your house to say this in person, but given the circumstances and my condition, I'm not allowed to leave the room, not even to use the bathroom. It's not my intention to make you or anyone else feel pity, and I don't want you to feel guilty. I'm writing to let you know I'm releasing you, I'm amputating you. Be happy and never seek me again. I don't want to hear from you, I don't want you to hear from me. If there is anything I'd enjoy before I die, it'd be not having to see your fucking horrible bastard face wandering around my garden.

That is all, I can now go to be chopped up in peace.

Good bye from somebody who is crazy and vehemently in love with you,

Your Frida

LETTER 25
AWAY FROM YOU I AM AS NOTHING
Lester Halbreich to Shirley Halbreich
August 1944

Lester Halbreich and Shirley Scheller met in 1941 at the
Stevensille Hotel in the Catskills, New York, when
Lester, a waiter, was looking after the table of Shirley
and her holidaying family. Four months later, on 24
December, they were married; but by that point,
everything had changed for the Halbreichs, and indeed
countless others, with Japan's military strike on Pearl
Harbor. The attack led to the US becoming involved in
World War II the following day and Lester being called
up for service in the Navy. For the eighteen months
that he did serve, Lester and Shirley wrote to each
other almost daily – by the time he returned home,
approximately 600 letters had been exchanged, many
of which were later published by their daughter. One
Sunday evening in August 1944, missing her more than
usual, Lester poured his heart out on paper.

THE LETTER

August, 1944
(1100 Sunday night)

My Darling Wife,
And I mean my darling wife. My roommate is reading right now, so I am ready to sit up for a few minutes and write to you to tell you how much I love you, and how much you mean to me.

I know that I've told you this a thousand or more times, but it bears repetition. I love you, my darling, with all my heart and with all my soul and with all my might. As I sit here typing this, I have both your pictures in front of me, and my heart goes out to you in the deepest of passion, and I could die of unrequited love because you are not here with me.

All day I've missed you. I've tried to fill in the void. I've played checkers, bowled, gone to the movies, drunk beer with the fellows, laughed and kidded (as best as I could), but all the time there was that great emptiness which nothing but the feel of you in my arms, and pressed close to me can fill. I miss the warmth of your lips against mine, the nearness of you to me in every way. I am frightfully and desperately lonely for you . . . and I am glad; glad because I know you miss me as greatly as I do you; and glad in the anticipation of our reunion.

Oh, darling, how lucky we are to love one another. Every day (or almost every day) I meet people who are married and not in love, and what does life hold for them. Nothing. But for you and I my sweetest darling, life holds everything. Why, only the prospect of being together with you makes it worthwhile.

I don't apologize for being passionate. I feel passionate. If I had you with me now I would love you passionately (as I could love only you amongst all the women in the world, and as you could love only me). All day long I've sat thinking of you. I tried to call you this evening, but there was too long a delay so I sit down to you and send myself to you as best I can via a typewriter.

I won't write this way again soon, my life, my excuse for living, but this once I had to let all the love I feel for you pour out unstinted.

I love you. You are my "raison d'être." Without you, life is meaningless; with you it is a perfect sonnet, a fine-cut gem, a beautifully conceived symphony. Or to descend to the other end of the ladder of words, I was no damned good before I met you. And life is only worthwhile while I am with you. Away from you I am as nothing. How well this has been shown in the last month.

I could rave more. Indeed, darling, that is what I want to do. To sit here and look at your picture, and drink in your beauty of soul and body, and revel in the thought that as I love you so do you love me; but rapt as I am in thoughts of you, the wishes of three roommates must be respected, and they want to sleep. So, goodnight, my dearest love, sleep well, and think of me, please, each night, before falling to sleep, as I do of thee.

Love,

Les

LETTER 26

A THOUSAND KISSES AS FIERY AS MY SOUL

Napoléon Bonaparte to Joséphine de Beauharnais

19 July 1796

*Born in Corsica in 1769, Napoléon Bonaparte is
considered one of history's most effective and powerful
military leaders, and a strategist with no equal. His
rise was swift, and in 1804, having led the French
campaign in Egypt and Syria, he was crowned Emperor
of the French; the next year, he was King of Italy. In
1795, as he began to climb the ranks, he met and
fell in love with Joséphine de Beauharnais, and within
months had proposed marriage: in March 1796,
forty-eight hours after their wedding, he left her and
led the French army to war. Napoléon was an avid
correspondent and, even when deep in conflict,
somehow managed to write countless love letters
to his wife. He was also incredibly impatient, and
regularly despaired on days when a reply from
Joséphine failed to appear, such as 19 July 1796.*

THE LETTER

Marmirolo, July 19, 1796

I have been without letters from you for two days.
That is at least the thirtieth time to-day that I have
made this observation to myself; you are thinking
this particularly wearisome; yet you cannot doubt
the tender and unique anxiety with which you
inspire me.

We attacked Mantua yesterday. We warmed it up
from two batteries with red-hot shot and from
mortars. All night long that wretched town has
been on fire. The sight was horrible and majestic.
We have secured several of the outworks; we open
the first parallel to-night. To-morrow I start for
Castiglione with the Staff, and I reckon on sleeping
there. I have received a courier from Paris. There
were two letters for you; I have read them. But
though this action appears to me quite natural, and
though you gave me permission to do so the other
day, I fear you may be vexed, and that is a great
trouble to me. I should have liked to have sealed
them up again: fie! that would have been atrocious.
If I am to blame, I beg your forgiveness. I swear
that it is not because I am jealous; assuredly not. I
have too high an opinion of my beloved for that.

I should like you to give me full permission to read your letters, then there would be no longer either remorse or apprehension.

Achille has just ridden post from Milan; no letters from my beloved! Adieu, my unique joy. When will you be able to rejoin me? I shall have to fetch you myself from Milan.

A thousand kisses as fiery as my soul, as chaste as yourself.

I have summoned the courier; he tells me that he crossed over to your house, and that you told him you had no commands. Fie! naughty, un-dutiful, cruel, tyrannous, jolly little monster. You laugh at my threats, at my infatuation; ah, you well know that if I could shut you up in my breast, I would put you in prison there!

Tell me you are cheerful, in good health, and very affectionate

Bonaparte

'AH, YOU WELL KNOW
THAT IF I COULD SHUT
YOU UP IN MY BREAST,
I WOULD PUT YOU IN
PRISON THERE!'
— Napoléon Bonaparte

LETTER 27
GOOD LUCK, MY DARLING
Nelson Mandela to Winnie Mandela
23 June 1969

Decades before Nelson Mandela became South Africa's first black president, and a year after they first laid eyes on each other, Nelson Mandela married Winnie Madikizela. They remained together for thirty-eight long, often dark years – both personally and politically. Just five years after tying the knot, Nelson was incarcerated for a total of twenty-seven years in his home country as a result of his anti-apartheid activism – eighteen of which were spent in a cell measuring eight by seven feet on Robben Island, with little outside contact. It was there, in 1969, that he was informed Winnie had also been detained for sixteen months. Their only means of communication during their concurrent sentences was the letter, some of which failed to reach the recipient. It is unknown whether this one, written by Nelson in June of 1969, made its way through.

THE LETTER

My Darling,

One of my precious possessions here is the first
letter you wrote me on Dec. 20, 1962, shortly after
my first conviction. During the last 6 ½ years I
have read it over and over again & the sentiments
it expresses are as golden & fresh now as they
were the day I received it. With the aspirations &
views that you hold & the role you are playing in
the current battle of ideas, I have always known
that you would be arrested sooner or later. But
considering all that I have gone through, I had
somehow vaguely hoped that such a calamity
would be deferred & that you would be spared the
misfortune & misery of prison life. Accordingly
when the news of your arrest reached me on
May 17, in the midst of feverish preparations for
my finals, then only 25 days away, I was quite
unprepared & felt cold & lonely. That you were
free & able within limits to move about meant
much to me. I looked forward to all your visits
& to those of members of the family & friends
which you organised with your characteristic
ability & enthusiasm, to the lovely birthday,

wedding anniversary & Xmas cards which you never failed to send, & to the funds which in spite of difficulties you managed to raise. What made the disaster even more shattering was the fact that you had last visited me on Dec. 21 & I was actually expecting you to come down last month or in June. I was also awaiting your reply to my letter of Apr. 2 in which I discussed your illness & made suggestions.

For some time after receiving the news my faculties seemed to have ceased functioning & I turned almost instinctively to your letter as I have always done in the past whenever my resolution flagged or whenever I wanted to take away my mind from nagging problems:

"Most people do not realise that your physical presence would have meant nothing to me if the ideals for which you have dedicated your life have not been realised. I find living in hope the most wonderful thing. Our short lives together, my love, have always been full of expectation . . . In these hectic & violent years I have grown to love you more than I ever did before . . . Nothing can be as valuable as being part & parcel of the formation of the history of a country."

These are some of the gems this marvellous letter contains & after going through it on May 17

I felt once more on top of the world. Disasters will always come & go, leaving their victims either completely broken or steeled & seasoned & better able to face the next crop of challenges that may occur. It is precisely at the present moment that you should remember that hope is a powerful weapon & one no power on earth can deprive you of; & that nothing can be as valuable as being part & parcel of the history of a country. Permanent values in social life & thought cannot be created by people who are indifferent or hostile to the true aspirations of a nation. For one thing those who have no soul, no sense of national pride & no ideals to win can suffer neither humiliation nor defeat; they can evolve no national heritage, are inspired by no sacred mission & can produce no martyrs or national heroes. A new world will be won not by those who stand at a distance with their arms folded, but by those who are in the arena, whose garments are torn by storms & whose bodies are maimed in the course of contest. Honour belongs to those who never forsake the truth even when things seem dark & grim, who try over & over again, who are never discouraged by insults, humiliation & even defeat. Since the dawn of history, mankind has honoured & respected brave & honest people, men & women like you darling – an ordinary girl who hails from a country village hardly shown in most maps, wife of a kraal, which is the humblest even by peasant standards.

My sense of devotion to you precludes me from saying more in public than I have already done in this note which must pass through many hands. One day we will have the privacy which will enable us to share the tender thoughts which we have kept buried in our hearts during the past eight years.

In due course you will be charged & probably convicted. I suggest that you discuss matters with Niki immediately you are charged & make the necessary arrangements for funds for purposes of study, toilet, Xmas groceries & other personal expenses. You must also arrange for her to send you as soon as you are convicted photos with suitable leather picture frames. From experience I have found that a family photo is everything in prison & you must have it right from the beginning. From this side you will have all my monthly letters, darling. I have written a long letter to Zeni & Zindzi, care of Niki, explaining the position in an attempt to keep them informed & cheerful. I only hope they received my earlier letter of Feb. 4. Last month I wrote to Mummy at Bizana & to Sidumo.

This month I will write to Telli & to Uncle Marsh. I have heard neither from Kgatho, Maki, Wonga, Sef, Gibson, Lily, Mthetho & Amina to whom I wrote between Dec. & April.

It has been possible to write this letter by kind permission of Brig. Aucamp & I am sure he will be anxious to help you should you desire to reply to this letter whilst you are still under detention. If you succeed, please confirm whether you received my April letter. Meanwhile, I should like you to know that I am thinking of you every moment of the day. Good luck, my darling. A million kisses & tons & tons of love.

Devotedly,

Dalibunga

LETTER 28
I LOVE JUNE CARTER, I DO
Johnny Cash to June Carter
23 June 1994

Country singers Johnny Cash and June Carter first crossed each other's paths at a gig in 1956, and, despite Cash already being married, the connection was instant. Cash proposed to Carter on more than one occasion, to no avail, but on 1 March 1968, thirteen years after first meeting and just a week after he proposed to her on stage during a concert, they finally married, remaining together until her death thirty-five years later. In 1994, on the occasion of June's sixty-fifth birthday, Johnny wrote her a letter. It would be another nine years until she passed away. Soon afterwards, he wrote another note.

THE LETTER

Happy Birthday Princess,
We get old and get used to each other. We think
alike. We read each others minds. We know what
the other wants without asking. Sometimes we
irritate each other a little bit. Maybe sometimes
take each other for granted.

But once in awhile, like today, I meditate on it
and realize how lucky I am to share my life with
the greatest woman I ever met. You still fascinate
and inspire me. You influence me for the better.
You're the object of my desire, the #1 Earthly
reason for my existence. I love you very much.

Happy Birthday Princess.
John

July 11 2003
Noon

I love June Carter, I do. Yes I do. I love June Carter I
do. And she loves me.

But now she's an angel and I'm not. Now she's
an angel and I'm not.

LETTER 29
A SQUEAL OF PAIN
Vita Sackville-West to Virginia Woolf
22 January 1926

Prominent English novelist Vita Sackville-West's
marriage to Sir Harold Nicolson was the very definition
of an open one, with both partners happily enjoying
same-sex, extramarital relationships for much of the
forty-nine years they spent together. In the early 1920s
Vita began what was to be her most famous affair,
with Virginia Woolf, the hugely influential author
responsible for such classics as Mrs Dalloway *and*
Orlando, *the latter of which was inspired, in part, by*
Vita's life. In January 1926 Vita reluctantly departed
London to join her husband, then a diplomat working
in Persia, for four long months; on the twenty-first, as
she travelled by train, Vita wrote a longing letter to
the lover she had left behind.

THE LETTER

Milan

January 21

I am reduced to a thing that wants Virginia. I
composed a beautiful letter to you in the sleepless
nightmare hours of the night, and it has all
gone: I just miss you, in a quite simple desperate
human way. You, with all your un-dumb letters,
would never write so elementary a phrase as that;
perhaps you wouldn't even feel it. And yet I
believe you'll be sensible of a little gap. But you'd
clothe it in so exquisite a phrase that it would
lose a little of its reality. Whereas with me it is
quite stark: I miss you even more than I could
have believed; and I was prepared to miss you a
good deal. So this letter is just really a squeal of
pain. It is incredible how essential to me you
have become. I suppose you are accustomed to
people saying these things. Damn you, spoilt
creature; I shan't make you love me any the more
by giving myself away like this—But oh my dear,
I *can't* be clever and stand-offish with you: I
love you too much for that. Too truly. You have no
idea how stand-offish I can be with people I don't
love. I have brought it to a fine art. But you have

broken down my defences. And I don't really resent
it.

However I won't bore you with any more.

We have re-started, and the train is shaky again.
I shall have to write at the stations – which are
fortunately many across the Lombard plain.

Venice. The stations were many, but I didn't
bargain for the Orient Express not stopping at
them. And here we are at Venice for ten minutes
only,—a wretched time in which to try and write.
No time to buy an Italian stamp even, so this will
have to go from Trieste.

The waterfalls in Switzerland were frozen into
solid iridescent curtains of ice, hanging over the
rock; so lovely. And Italy all blanketed in snow.

We're going to start again. I shall have to wait
till Trieste tomorrow morning. Please forgive me for
writing such a miserable letter.

V.

'I AM REDUCED TO A
THING THAT WANTS
VIRGINIA.'

— *Vita Sackville-West*

LETTER 30
I SHALL ALWAYS BE NEAR YOU
Sullivan Ballou to Sarah Ballou
14 July 1861

*In 1861, as the American Civil War approached, a
thirty-two-year-old lawyer named Sullivan Ballou left
his wife of five years and two sons at home, and
joined the war effort as a major in the Union Army.
On 14 July that year, acutely aware that particularly
perilous times were ahead, he wrote, but didn't send,
the following beautiful letter to his wife, in which he
eloquently warned her of the dangers he faced and
spoke of his love for both his family and country.
Sadly, two weeks after penning his letter, Sullivan was
killed in the First Battle of Bull Run – the first major
conflict of a war that lasted four years and cost the
lives of approximately 750,000 people – along with
ninety-three of his men. The letter was later found
amongst his belongings and then delivered to his
widow, but has since been lost. This copy, thought to
have been transcribed by a relative, is held at the
Abraham Lincoln Presidential Library.*

*Sarah, who was twenty-four when he died, never
remarried. She passed away at eighty years of age,
and is now buried alongside her husband in
Providence, Rhode Island.*

THE LETTER

Headquarters
Camp Clark
Washington D. C.
July 14th 1861

My Very dear Wife

The indications are very strong that we shall move
in a few days perhaps tomorrow and lest I should
not be able to write you again I feel impelled to
write a few lines that may fall under your eye
when I am no more. Our movement may be one
of a few days duration and be full of pleasure. And
it may be one of severe conflict and death to me
"Not my will but thine O God be done" if it is
necessary that I should fall, on the battle field for
my Country I am ready. I have no misgivings about
or lack of confidence in the Cause in which I am
engaged, and my courage does not halt or falter. I
know how American Civilization now leans upon
the triumph of the Government and how great a
debt we owe to those who went before us through
the blood and suffering of the Revolution; and I
am willing perfectly willing to lay down all my
joys in this life to help maintain this Government
and to pay that debt.

But my dear wife, when I know that with my own joys I lay down nearly all of yours, – and replace them in this life with care and sorrow when after having eaten for long years the bitter fruit of orphanage myself, I must offer it as their only sustenance to my dear little children, is it weak or dishonourable that while the banner of purpose flotes calmly and proudly in the breeze, underneath my unbounded love for you my dear wife and children should struggle in fierce though useless contest with my love of Country

I cannot describe to you my feelings on this calm summer night when two thousand men are sleeping around me, many of them enjoying the last perhaps before that of Death. And I suspicious that Death is creeping behind me with his fatal dart am communing with God my Country and thee. I have sought most closely and diligently and often in my brest for a wrong motive in thus hazarding the happiness of all that I love and I could not find one. A pure love of my Country and of the principels I have advocated before the people and the name of honour that I love more than I fear death, have called upon me and I have obeyed.

Sarah my love for you is deathless it seemes to bind me with Mighty Cables that nothing but Omnipotence can break. And yet my love of

Country comes over me like a strong wind and
bears me irresistibly with all those chains to the
battle field the memories of all the blissful moments
I have enjoyed with you come crouding over me,
and I feel most deeply grateful to God and you that
I have enjoyed them so long. And how hard it is for
me to give them up; and burn to ashes the hopes
of future years when God willing we might still
have loved and loved together and see our boys
grow up to honourable manhood around us. I know
I have but few claimes upon Divine Providence but
something whispers to me perhaps it is the wafted
prayer of my little Edgar that I shall return to my
loved ones unharmed. If I do not my dear Sarah
never forget how much I loved you nor that when
my last breath escapes me on the battlefield it will
whisper your name

Forgive my many faults and the many pains I
have caused you. How thoughtless how foolish I
have sometimes been! How gladly would I wash out
with my tears every little spot upon your happiness
and strugle with all the misfortunes of this world to
shield you and my children from harm but I cannot
I must watch you from the spirit world and hover
near you while you buffet the stormes with your
precious little freight – and wait with sad paitience
till we meet to part no more

But Oh Sarah! if the dead can come back to this earth and flit unseen around those they love I shall be always with you in the brightest day and the darkest night amidst your happiest sceans and gloomiest hours always always and when the soft breeze fans your cheek it shall be my breath or the cool air your throbbing temple it shall be my spirit passing by. Sarah, do not mourn me dead think I am gone and wait for me for we shall meet again.

As for my little boys they will grow up as I have done and never know a fathers love and care.

Little Willie is to young to remember me long but my blue eyed Edgar will keep my frolics with him among the dimmest memories of his childhood

Sarah I have unlimited confidence in your maternal care and your development of their characters. Tell my two Mothers I call Gods blessings upon them

Oh! Sarah I wait for you then come to me and lead thither my children

Sullivan

'MY LOVE FOR YOU IS
DEATHLESS IT SEEMES TO
BIND ME WITH MIGHTY
CABLES THAT NOTHING
BUT OMNIPOTENCE
CAN BREAK'
— Sullivan Ballou

PERMISSION CREDITS

Every effort has been made to trace copyright holders and obtain their permission for the use of copyright material. The publisher apologises for any errors or omissions and would be grateful if notified of any corrections that should be incorporated in future reprints or editions of this book.

LETTER 1 '11/10/58 letter to Thom Steinbeck' by John Steinbeck, copyright © 1952 by John Steinbeck, © 1969 by The Estate of John Steinbeck, © 1975 by Elaine A. Steinbeck and Robert Wallsten; from *Steinbeck: A Life in Letters* by John Steinbeck, edited by Elaine Steinbeck and Robert Wallsten. Used by permission of Viking Books, an imprint of Penguin Publishing Group, a division of Penguin Random House LLC. All rights reserved / Reproduced with permission of Curtis Brown Group Ltd, on behalf of the Estate of John Steinbeck / Copyright © 1952 by John Steinbeck Copyright © Executors of the Estate of John Steinbeck, 1969. Reprinted with permission of McIntosh & Otis, Inc. / 387 words from *A Life in Letters* by John Steinbeck (Penguin Classics, 2001). Copyright © Elaine A. Steinbeck and Robert Wallsten 1975.
LETTER 2 from *Lettres à Nelson Algren 1947–1964* © Editions Gallimard 1997.
LETTER 3 by kind permission of Martha Freeman, granddaughter of Dorothy Freeman and editor of *Always, Rachel: The Letters of Rachel Carson and Dorothy Freeman, 1952–1964*.
LETTER 6 Copyright © 2014, The Estate of Vladimir Nabokov, used by permission of The Wylie Agency (UK) Limited / *Briefe an Véra* by Nabokov, Vladimir / Übersetzt von Tolksdorf, Ludger; Herausgegeben von Boyd, Brian; Herausgegeben von Voronina, Olga © 2017, Rowohlt Verlag GmbH, Hamburg / Lettera di Vladimir Nabokov a Vera ristampata con il permesso di Adelphi Edizioni S.p.A / © Librairie Arthème Fayard, 2017 / 837 words from *Letters to Vera* by Vladimir Nabokov. Copyright © The Estate of Vladimir Nabokov, 2014. Introduction and Appendix Two © Brian Boyd, 2014. Translator's Note © Olga Voronina, 2014 / Excerpt(s) from *Letters to Vera* by Vladimir Nabokov, edited and translated by Olga Voronina and Brian Boyd, compilation copyright © 2014 by The Estate of Vladimir Nabokov. Used by permission of Alfred A. Knopf, an imprint of the Knopf Doubleday Publishing Group, a division of Penguin Random House LLC. All rights reserved.
LETTER 7 'Paris, July 26, 1908', from *The Gonne-Yeats Letters 1893–1938* by Anna MacBride White and A. Norman Jeffares. Copyright © 1992 by Anna MacBride White and A. Norman Jeffares.

ACKNOWLEDGEMENTS

It requires a dedicated team of incredibly patient people to bring the *Letters of Note* books to life, and this page serves as a heartfelt thank you to every single one of them, beginning with my wife, Karina — not just for kickstarting my obsession with letters all those years ago, but for working with me as Permissions Editor, a vital and complex role. Special mention, also, to my excellent editor at Canongate Books, Hannah Knowles, who has somehow managed to stay focused despite the problems I have continued to throw her way.

Equally sincere thanks to all of the following: the one and only Jamie Byng, whose vision and enthusiasm for this series has proven invaluable; all at Canongate Books, including but not limited to Rafi Romaya, Kate Gibb, Vicki Rutherford and Leila Cruickshank; my dear family at Letters Live: Jamie, Adam Ackland, Benedict Cumberbatch, Aimie Sullivan, Amelia Richards and Nick Allott; my agent, Caroline Michel, and everyone else at Peters, Fraser & Dunlop; the many illustrators who have worked on the beautiful covers in this series; the talented performers who have lent their stunning voices not just to Letters Live, but also to the *Letters of Note* audiobooks; Patti Pirooz; every single archivist and librarian in the world; everyone at Unbound; the team at the Wylie Agency for their assistance and understanding; my foreign publishers for their continued support; and, crucially, my family, for putting up with me during this process.

Finally, and most importantly, thank you to all of the letter writers whose words feature in these books.